My Guide to the
CONSTITUTION

THE
BILL OF
RIGHTS

Amie Jane Leavitt

Mitchell Lane
PUBLISHERS
P.O. Box 196
Hockessin, Delaware 19707

My Guide to the
CONSTITUTION

THE BILL OF RIGHTS
THE EXECUTIVE BRANCH
THE JUDICIAL BRANCH
THE LEGISLATIVE BRANCH
THE POWER OF THE STATES
THE STORY OF THE CONSTITUTION

Copyright © 2012 by Mitchell Lane Publishers

Printing   1   2   3   4   5   6   7   8   9

All rights reserved. No part of this book may be reproduced without written permission from the publisher. Printed and bound in the United States of America.

PUBLISHER'S NOTE: The Constitution of the United States appears in the appendix to My Guide to the Constitution: *The Story of the Constitution.* The amendments to the Constitution, including the Bill of Rights, appear in the appendix to this book.

    The facts on which the story in this book is based have been thoroughly researched. Documentation of such research can be found on page 44. While every possible effort has been made to ensure accuracy, the publisher will not assume liability for damages caused by inaccuracies in the data, and makes no warranty on the accuracy of the information contained herein. The information contained herein should not be taken as legal advice. For any legal questions, please contact an attorney.

**Library of Congress
Cataloging-in-Publication Data**
Leavitt, Amie Jane.
  The Bill of Rights / by Amie Jane Leavitt.
    p. cm.—(My guide to the Constitution)
  Includes bibliographical references and index.
  ISBN 978-1-58415-947-6 (library bound)
  1. United States. Constitution. 1st–10th Amendments—History—Juvenile literature. 2. Constitutional amendments—United States—History—Juvenile literature. 3. Civil rights—United States—Juvenile literature. I. Title.
  KF4750.L429 2011
  342.7308'5—dc22
                               2011000611

Paperback ISBN: 9781612281896

eBook ISBN: 9781612280912

PLB

CONTENTS

Chapter One
  A New Government 4

Chapter Two
  Freedom to Believe, Speak, Worship, and Assemble 10

Chapter Three
  Protecting Our Lives and Our Property 18

Chapter Four
  Trials, Punishments, and Rights Not Mentioned.............. 26

Chapter Five
  Preservation and Promotion 32

Appendix: Amendments to the Constitution 38

Further Reading.. 44

  Books 44

  Works Consulted 44

  On the Internet 45

Glossary... 46

Index 47

Words in **bold** type can be found in the glossary.

Chapter 1

A New Government

Only four years had passed since the end of the Revolutionary War, yet during the hot summer of 1787, leaders of the states were already meeting to discuss a dramatic change in the government. In 1776, during the Revolutionary War, they had written a document called the Articles of Confederation. It explained how the government of the colonies would be organized and how laws would be made. After the war, it became clear that the government described in the Articles would not work for the new nation. It was the responsibility of these leaders—including George Washington, James Madison, Alexander Hamilton, George Mason, and Benjamin Franklin—to agree on how the government of the newly formed United States should be run.

Hot Topics
The Constitutional Convention lasted from May until September of 1787. During that time, the leaders

Farmers and Minutemen faced the
British in the Battle at Lexington
Green, 1775. With this "shot heard
'round the world," the revolution
began, leading to a new government.

discussed many important ideas and issues. In their discussions, they sought to answer many questions, such as:

- Who should have more power, the national government or the states?
- How should presidents be elected?
- How should leaders in Congress be elected and how long should they serve?
- Who should have the right to vote?

For each of these questions and all the others that were talked about at the convention, there were many different answers and opinions. After much debate, however, a **consensus**—or agreement—was finally made on many of them. The **delegates'** final agreement became known as the U.S. **Constitution.**

The Rights of the People
Most of the important questions were agreed upon before the Constitution was finished. Surprisingly, one big question was not: "Should the Constitution protect the rights of the people?"

All the leaders at the convention agreed that the rights of people should be protected. After all, a democracy is by definition a government for and of the people. It was because England's King George III abused the rights of the colonists during his rule that they had sought independence during the Revolutionary War. Two opposing groups had strong opinions about why the rights of the people should or should not be in the Constitution.

One group of leaders, called the **Federalists,** did not think it was necessary to include a list of rights in the Constitution. In fact, the Federalists feared that by including some rights and not others, the government could actually limit the rights of the people. Another group of leaders, called the **Antifederalists,** believed the opposite. They felt that if the rights weren't listed in the Constitution, then the government

During King George's rule of the colonies, British sailors would force colonists to serve in the British navy. Called impressment, the practice was one of the ways the king abused individual rights.

would have the power to take away these rights at any time. By listing them in the Constitution, the rights of the people would be guaranteed and protected.

Most people in the country agreed with the second group of leaders. They remembered what it felt like to have limited rights under King George's rule, and they didn't want that to happen to them again. They wanted a Bill of Rights included in the Constitution.

When the Constitution was sent to the states for **ratification,** many of the states voiced this opinion. New York, Massachusetts, and Virginia said they wanted a Bill of Rights. They even came up with their own lists of suggestions for the delegates to include. North Carolina and Rhode Island believed so strongly that the Constitution should have a Bill of Rights that they would not approve the Constitution at all unless one was added.

James Madison, by
Gilbert Stuart, 1805

Drafting the Bill

Although James Madison was a Federalist, he was also a great writer. Because of this, he was placed on the committee to write the Bill of Rights.

Madison looked at many documents when he wrote his list of rights. He wanted to get ideas for what was important to people in his day and in the past. One was the Magna Carta, which was written in England in 1215. Another was the English Bill of Rights, which was written in 1689. He also looked at the lists that were written by some of the states, such as the Virginia Declaration of Rights, written by George Mason in 1776. All of these documents helped Madison come up with a list of rights that he thought would be important to the people of the United States.

By the time Congress met in 1789, Madison had a list of seventeen rights. The leaders in Congress talked about each one. They decided whether each was important or not, and if it was, why it was important. Finally, after talking about the list for the entire summer of 1789, Congress had agreed on twelve **amendments** to be added to the Constitution.

Before anything could be added to the Constitution, though, it had to be approved by the states. The delegates took the list to each of their state **legislatures,** where the amendments were debated again. In the end, not all twelve amendments were approved—the original

Ratification Dates of the Bill of Rights		
STATE	DATE	VOTE
New Jersey	November 20, 1789	Rejected amendment 2
Maryland	December 19, 1789	Approved all amendments
North Carolina	December 22, 1789	Approved all amendments
South Carolina	January 19, 1790	Approved all amendments
New Hampshire	January 25, 1790	Rejected amendment 2
Delaware	January 28, 1790	Rejected amendment 1
New York	February 27, 1790	Rejected amendment 2
Pennsylvania	March 10, 1790	Rejected amendment 2
Rhode Island	June 7, 1790	Rejected amendment 2
Vermont	November 3, 1791	Approved all amendments
Virginia	December 15, 1791	Approved all amendments

amendments 1 and 2 were rejected. The original amendment 3 became amendment 1.

New Jersey was the first state to approve the ten amendments, and Virginia was the eleventh—the last one needed for ratification. These first ten amendments to the Constitution have been known ever since as the Bill of Rights.

Only 11 states needed to approve the Bill of Rights for it to be ratified. Massachusetts, Connecticut, and Georgia did not vote to ratify the document until 1939, when the Bill of Rights was 150 years old. Vermont had become a state less than a year before ratification—on March 4, 1791.

One of the two amendments that did not make it into the Bill of Rights was never added to the Constitution. The other was added centuries later—in 1992. It is the 27th Amendment, which states that members of Congress cannot change their rate of pay for the current term.

Chapter 2

Freedom to Believe, Speak, Worship, and Assemble

Have you ever wondered what it might be like to live in a place where you were only allowed to say, do, and believe things that a government agreed with? Believe it or not, many people today live in places that are like this. The first amendment in the Bill of Rights gives U.S. citizens the right to speak, write, worship, and assemble without fear of punishment.

Freedom of Speech

In October 2010, a woman in China added a comment and retweeted her fiancé's Twitter post. He had written about a Chinese protest against Japan; she had jokingly added the words, "Charge, angry youth." Eleven days later—on the day they had planned to marry—both the woman and her fiancé were arrested. The fiancé was released five days later, but the woman was sentenced to one year in a labor camp. Her crime: disturbing social stability.

It is this exact type of situation that the framers of the Constitution feared. They did not ever want the

Freedom of Religion

One of the reasons early settlers moved from Europe to North America was for freedom of religion. The Pilgrims, for example, were not allowed to practice their religion freely in England. If they did, they faced persecution and sometimes imprisonment. They left their homes and braved the dangers of the New World so that they could worship without fear of punishment. In 1620, they founded Plymouth Colony.

Quakers came to Pennsylvania, a colony that William Penn set up for them in 1682. Many Catholics settled in Maryland because Lord Baltimore had founded the colony to protect those who believed in that faith.

The First Amendment actually protects several ideas associated with freedom of religion. First, it says: "Congress shall make no law respecting an establishment of religion." This means that the U.S. government cannot make laws about religion. It also means that the government cannot make a "state religion" or say that everyone must follow a certain religion.

The second part says: "or prohibiting the free exercise thereof." This simply means that the government cannot keep people from practicing their religion. The Constitution lets people believe in whatever religion they want to, and it protects people who don't want to practice any religion at all. Because the government may not interfere with religious worship, the United States enjoys "separation of church and state."

Freedom of the Press

"Freedom of the press" refers to the printing press. It is the freedom to print people's ideas in magazines, newspapers, books, and other forms of media. People in the United States can read different ideas and viewpoints in newspapers or on the Internet. They can listen to news reporters describing events on television. Since things have always been that way in the United States, it may not sound like an important right, but there are many cases where people who have not had this right have suffered.

For example, just one month after Adolf Hitler rose to power in Germany, the lives of Germans began to change. It was February 1933, and a fire had broken out in an important government building. Even though no one knew for sure who had started the fire, the **Nazis** believed it was a group of communists trying to take over the government. Hitler and the other Nazi leaders said they had to act quickly to protect Germany and its people.

They changed the country's constitution and took away the civil liberties of the German people. Germans could no longer express their opinions. They could no longer write and print their ideas and beliefs. They could no longer gather in groups. They could no longer talk on the telephone or send mail without the government being able to listen in or read their words. The government could search their houses whenever they wanted and take anything they wanted. These new laws gave the Nazis almost unlimited power. They could now persecute and harm groups of people without technically breaking any German laws.

In February 1933, arsons set fire to the Reichstag—the German parliamentary building. Because of this event, the Nazis drastically changed the German constitution and severely limited the rights of the people.

The National Archives in
Washington, D.C.

The Bill of Rights, along with the Constitution of the United States and the Declaration of Independence, are known as the Charters of Freedom, and they permanently reside in the Rotunda for the Charters of Freedom in the National Archives in Washington, D.C. The Charters were placed there in 1952 when the National Archives received charge of them from the Library of Congress.

temperature control to protect the document from extreme heat and humidity.

The light inside the Charters of Freedom cases looks greenish blue. Normal light will harm the documents over time, causing the ink to fade. If the documents weren't placed under these special lights, the ink would fade so much that eventually we wouldn't be able to read them at all. For the same reason, people are no longer allowed to use flash photography inside the National Archives. The flash from cameras will damage the documents, too. At night, the cases are lowered into underground vaults.

If you don't live near Washington, D.C., and don't think you'll be able to visit the National Archives in person, you can still see the documents online. The archive has a web site that shows pictures of the documents and explains more about them and their importance to U.S. history.

Global Impact of the Bill of Rights

The Bill of Rights, one of the most important documents in the U.S. government, has protected the rights of Americans for more than 200 years. Because it has been so successful, it has been used as the basis for similar bills of rights for other countries and for international law.

International Law

Because of the human rights violations that happened during World War II, after the war the leaders of the victorious nations agreed that a Bill of Rights was necessary for all people everywhere. The United Nations was established in 1945 in order to curb warfare and to protect human rights around the world. In December 1948, the General

The United Nations Building (foreground) is located on the east side of New York's island of Manhattan. Once you enter the United Nations' 18-acre property, you are no longer in the United States but are instead on international soil.

Assembly of the United Nations agreed on the Universal Declaration of Human Rights. It included 30 groups of rights, such as the following:

- Everyone has the right to life, liberty and security of person.
- No one shall be held in slavery.
- No one shall be subjected to torture or to cruel, inhuman or degrading treatment or punishment.
- Everyone has the right to recognition everywhere as a person before the law.
- No one shall be subjected to arbitrary arrest, detention or exile.
- Everyone is entitled in full equality to a fair and public hearing by an independent and impartial tribunal, in the determination of his rights and obligations and of any criminal charge against him.
- Everyone has the right to leave any country, including his own, and to return to his country.
- Everyone has the right to a nationality.

First Lady Eleanor Roosevelt holds a copy of the United Nations Universal Declaration of Human Rights written in Spanish.

Even the classic movie *King Kong* was censored twice in Germany. The film was banned outright by the Censorship Office in Berlin. In December 1933, it was allowed to be shown after many cuts, and it was released with the new title, *The Fable of King Kong — An American Trick and Sensational Film.*

After the Nazis changed their constitution, they used the press to further control the population. People could no longer read any news except what the Nazis wanted them to read. What the Nazis approved was usually false. The way the news was written made the Nazis and their views look good and right, while people from different ethnic, religious, and political groups were portrayed as evil and inhuman. They also controlled what was broadcast over the radio and what was shown at movie theaters. They burned books they didn't agree with, including religious books, and artwork they thought was inappropriate. These changes helped the Nazis

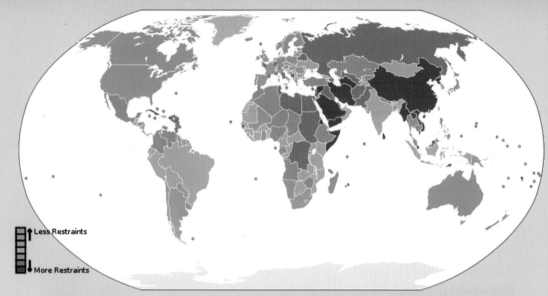

Chapter 2

Source: Reporters Without Borders

The colors on this map indicate which countries have the least and most restrictions on freedom of the press. If you live in a country that is shaded blue, your government does not limit the information you can read and write. If you live in a country shaded in red or orange, you are severely limited.

execute their plan of widespread persecution across Germany and the countries they conquered during World War II.

The Nazi government hasn't been the only one to try to control the press. Countries such as China, North Korea, Iran, and Vietnam do not allow freedom of the press for their people. Reporters Without Borders has assembled a map that shows what countries have the most and least restrictions on freedom of the press. The people who live in the countries in red and dark orange have very few freedoms to write what they want, and the government controls the information they receive.

Although people in the United States have the right to a free press, they do not have the right to print what they know is a lie. This type of writing is called **libel,** and because it can harm other people, it is against the law.

Freedom to Assemble

To assemble means "to gather in groups." With this freedom, people can get together with other people and talk about ideas. They can protest things they don't agree with—they just have to do so peacefully. Depending on where they want to gather, they may also need to get a permit.

Freedom to Petition the Government

If you live in the United States and the government does something you don't like, you can tell the government how you feel. You can write a letter to any leader and express your feelings.

In the 1700s, the colonists tried to do this when they disagreed with the laws of King George III. Instead of listening to their grievances, the king passed more laws to punish the colonists. Since the colonists didn't have any say in what laws were passed—they had no representatives in the British government—there was very little they could do. That was the main reason they fought for their freedom in the Revolutionary War.

Today, you can petition the government whenever you want. If you don't like something that has happened in your town, you can go to a city council meeting and speak in front of the leaders. You can also write a letter to the mayor and explain your views. Not only can you write to the leaders of your town, but you can also write or call the leaders of your county, state, or nation.

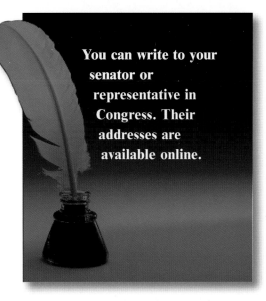

You can write to your senator or representative in Congress. Their addresses are available online.

Chapter 3

Protecting Our Lives and Our Property

Some people get confused when they first read the Second Amendment, which is about the right to "bear arms." The word *arms* has more than one meaning, and in this case, it means "guns or weapons." This amendment gives people the right to own and carry guns or weapons.

Amendment II

A well regulated Militia, being necessary to the security of a free State, the right of the people to keep and bear Arms, shall not be infringed.

This amendment is controversial. Some people believe that the framers intended for people to own guns only for the purpose of having an army ready to protect the state or the country. Others believe they intended for *everyone* to own weapons for personal protection as well. Some people don't think it's a

These smoothbore flintlock muskets are the type of guns that the patriots used while fighting for their freedom in the Revolutionary War.

The framers may not have thought that ordinary people might use guns for their own selfish reasons, like the infamous Bonnie and Clyde did when they robbed banks in the 1930s.

good idea for everyone to own guns. What about people who break the law and hurt other people with them?

Using a weapon while committing a crime is not protected under the Second Amendment. This amendment just gives people the right to own guns and other weapons; it does not say they can do anything they want with them. People who have been convicted of certain crimes may be denied the right to own a gun.

Amendment III

In the 1700s, many British soldiers lived in the colonies. The Redcoats, as they were called, were just about everywhere. Many of them were in North America to fight the French and Indian War, which was fought from 1754 to 1763. They stayed by order of the king.

Not only were the Redcoats roaming the streets of colonial towns, but they were also roaming the homes of the colonists and eating their food. Why? This was a right that they had. If a soldier came to the home of a colonist and wanted food and shelter, the colonist had to comply. Putting them up was called **quartering.** The king felt that since the soldiers were there to protect the colonists, the colonists were obligated to feed and house the soldiers.

Many colonists resented the quartering act. Imagine how you would feel. You have worked hard on your farm to grow food for your family. You have labored in the kitchen to prepare the food. Then, just when you're about to sit down for a family meal, a knock comes at the door. It's a group of hungry soldiers who push their way in and sit down at your table. They dig into your dinner, devouring every morsel they can find. When they are done, they lick their lips and kick their feet up on your bed and take a nap. Meanwhile, all that is left for you are a few scraps and a bunch of dirty dishes.

Not all soldiers behaved this way, but it happened often enough to make the colonists feel angry and frustrated. That's exactly why the framers included the Third Amendment in the Constitution.

Amendment III

No Soldier shall, in time of peace be quartered in any house, without the consent of the Owner, nor in time of war, but in a manner to be prescribed by law.

Amendment IV

Soldiers are not the only people who are not allowed to come into your home without your consent. Police officers may not enter, either—unless they have a search warrant. Search warrants are used when police officers believe someone is hiding clues to a crime, or hiding a criminal.

If a police officer has good reason ("probable cause") to believe that a criminal or evidence of a crime is inside someone's home or other piece of property, the officer will ask a judge for a search warrant. When the judge signs this piece of paper, police officers have the right to look through the person's property. They will say something like, "We have a search warrant which gives us the right to come inside and search your home" or other piece of property. However, they may only search and take what is specifically listed on the warrant.

Amendment IV
The right of the people to be secure in their persons, houses, papers, and effects, against unreasonable searches and seizures, shall not be violated, and no Warrants shall issue, but upon probable cause, supported by Oath or affirmation, and particularly describing the place to be searched, and the persons or things to be seized.

If a police dog signals that it has found something illegal, then the police have probable cause to obtain a search warrant.

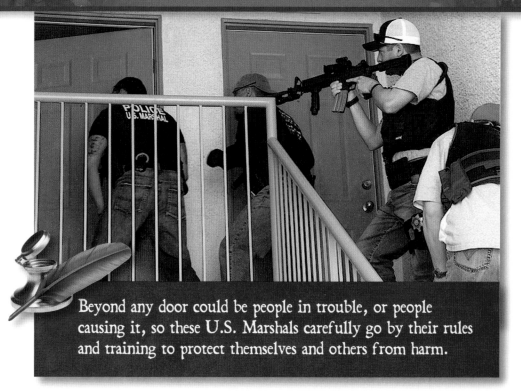

Beyond any door could be people in trouble, or people causing it, so these U.S. Marshals carefully go by their rules and training to protect themselves and others from harm.

While the Fourth Amendment guarantees that police officers cannot search a person's belongings without a search warrant, there are exceptions to this rule. For example, if a police officer believes that someone on private property is in danger, he or she may enter the property to protect that person.

Think about the example mentioned in chapter two about Nazi Germany. The right against unlawful searches and seizures was one of the rights the Germans lost when the Nazis changed that country's constitution. German police or Nazi soldiers could burst into someone's home and ransack the place, taking anything or anyone they wanted. This happened often in Nazi-occupied Europe during World War II. If the authorities found anything they didn't like, they could immediately arrest the people and take them away. If they found anything of value that they wanted, they could take it. Because the German constitution gave the authorities this power, the people could not do anything to protect themselves or their property from the people who were supposed to protect them.

A famous case of police brutality involved Rodney King, left, in 1991. King was beaten by Los Angeles police after he tried to outrun them. The beating was caught on videotape, and the resulting trials captured national attention. In the federal civil trial against the City of Los Angeles, King was awarded $3.8 million.

Amendment V

The Fifth Amendment of the U.S. Constitution also protects citizens from abuse by law enforcement officers or others in positions of authority.

Amendment V

No person shall be held to answer for a capital, or otherwise infamous crime, unless on a presentment or indictment of a Grand Jury, except in cases arising in the land or naval forces, or in the Militia, when in actual service in time of War or public danger; nor shall any person be subject for the same offence to be twice put in jeopardy of life or limb; nor shall be compelled in any criminal case to be a witness against himself, nor be deprived of life, liberty, or property, without due process of law; nor shall private property be taken for public use, without just compensation.

According to the Fifth Amendment, if the authorities think you committed a crime, they must follow a specific set of guidelines after they charge you:

1. If the crime is really serious, they must present their case before a **grand jury**. This is a group of citizens who listen to the case and decide if there is enough evidence to put you on trial.
2. Once you have gone on trial for a crime, you can't be charged with that exact crime again. Being tried twice for the same crime is called **double jeopardy**.
3. During your trial, you don't have to take the stand if you don't want to.
4. Even if the government thinks you have committed a crime, it cannot take away your life, liberty, or property without giving you a fair trial first.
5. If you have not been convicted of a crime and the government wants to take something that belongs to you, it must pay you for it.

The framers knew this amendment was very important. It would prevent the government from accusing and punishing people for crimes they did not commit.

Have you ever heard of someone "pleading the Fifth"? It means they are calling up the Fifth Amendment, which lets them remain quiet if what they say could make them sound guilty of a crime.

Chapter 4

Trials, Punishments, and Rights Not Mentioned

The U.S. legal system is based on the Fifth, Sixth, Seventh, and Eighth amendments. The Fifth Amendment is about the rules that must be followed when a person is charged with a crime. The Sixth Amendment talks about the trial itself.

Amendment VI

In all criminal prosecutions, the accused shall enjoy the right to a speedy and public trial, by an impartial jury of the State and district wherein the crime shall have been committed, which district shall have been previously ascertained by law, and to be informed of the nature and cause of the accusation; to be confronted with the witnesses against him; to have compulsory process for obtaining witnesses in his favor, and to have the Assistance of Counsel for his defence.

Speedy Trial. If you are charged with a crime, the Sixth Amendment gives you the right to a speedy

A district courthouse in Texas

trial. It might seem unnecessary to include the word *speedy*, but some governments have become famous for leaving accused criminals in jail for years and years before putting them on trial. Some people were never able to go to trial to prove their innocence. Because of the rights mentioned in the Sixth Amendment, the federal and local governments have to provide a trial in a fairly quick manner.

Public Trial. Not only does the trial have to be quick, it also has to be public. This is also very important, because authorities have the opportunity to be dishonest at trials held in secret.

Know What You Did Wrong. According to the Sixth Amendment, if you are arrested, you have the right to know why. The police can't just arrest you, toss you in jail, and never tell you what they are accusing you of doing.

Confront Witnesses. The Sixth Amendment gives you the right to confront the witnesses against you. If someone says that they saw you do something, you have the right to know who that person is and be able to have your lawyer ask the person questions in a trial.

Defense. The last part of the Sixth Amendment says that you have the right to have someone defend you in court. That "someone" is usually a lawyer, but you can also choose to defend yourself. If you want a lawyer but cannot afford one, a "public defender" may be assigned to your case. Public defenders are paid through the government.

Amendment VII
The Seventh Amendment gives people the right to a trial by **jury**. A jury is a group of **peers** who listen to the evidence in the trial and decide whether or not the accused person is guilty of the crime as charged.

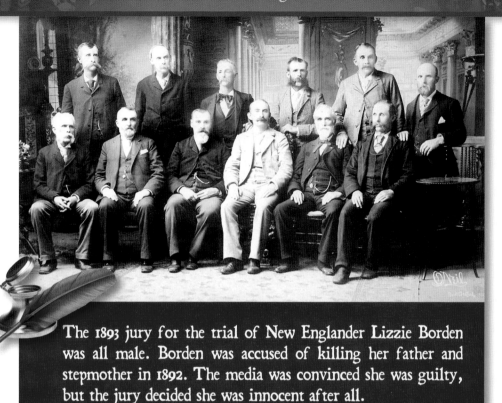

The 1893 jury for the trial of New Englander Lizzie Borden was all male. Borden was accused of killing her father and stepmother in 1892. The media was convinced she was guilty, but the jury decided she was innocent after all.

Amendment VII

In Suits at common law, where the value in controversy shall exceed twenty dollars, the right of trial by jury shall be preserved, and no fact tried by a jury, shall be otherwise re-examined in any Court of the United States, than according to the rules of the common law.

If a person did not have the right to a jury trial, he or she would have a trial decided by a judge instead. The framers did not want to give that power to one person. They realized it would be better to have a group of everyday people listening to the evidence against an accused person and deciding the **verdict.** In a jury trial, the jurors listen to the evidence. Then they go to a closed room and talk about what they heard. They decide whether the evidence proves the person's guilt as charged.

A bail bondsman may agree to pay people's bail to get them out of jail. If these people "jump bail" and don't show up to their trial, the bail bondsman will hunt them down and make them pay.

Amendment VIII

The Eighth Amendment has two parts. The first part is about **bail.** The second part is about punishment.

> **Amendment VIII**
> Excessive bail shall not be required, nor excessive fines imposed, nor cruel and unusual punishments inflicted.

Bail is money that can be paid to get someone out of jail until he or she goes to trial. The Eighth Amendment says that the amount of bail charged must not exceed the crime. For example, if a person is charged with a minor crime, the bail should be low. However, if a person is charged with a very serious crime, then the bail can be higher. Setting bail helps ensure that a person will not disappear before the trial. After he or she goes to trial, bail is refunded. People who "skip bail" lose the bail money.

The Eighth Amendment also protects people while they are imprisoned. It says that the government cannot do cruel things or order excessive punishments for those who are in jail. This amendment can be a little tricky. After all, what seems cruel to one person may not seem cruel to another. However, if it is proven that the authorities took away a person's Eighth Amendment rights, there can be serious consequences. Usually, treatment of prisoners in the United States is much better than in other countries—and that is because of the Eighth Amendment.

Amendment IX

Remember in chapter one the arguments that the Federalists had against including a Bill of Rights in the Constitution? They were afraid that if a right was not mentioned, then that right would not be protected. Since every single right could not possibly be mentioned in the Constitution, the Ninth Amendment covers that concern.

Amendment IX

The enumeration in the Constitution, of certain rights, shall not be construed to deny or disparage others retained by the people.

This amendment says that just because a right isn't mentioned in the Bill of Rights, it doesn't mean that the people don't have it.

Amendment X

The Tenth Amendment is the first amendment that talks about the rights of the government. This amendment simply says that if a power is not given to the national government, then it is given to the state governments or to the people. This applies only if that power is not outlawed in the Constitution.

Amendment X

The powers not delegated to the United States by the Constitution, nor prohibited by it to the States, are reserved to the States respectively, or to the people.

A bail bondsman is a person who makes a profit by posting bail for people who are accused of crimes. The United States is one of the few countries in the world that allows this profession.

Chapter **5**

Preservation and Promotion

When the Bill of Rights was originally added to the Constitution on December 15, 1791, fourteen handwritten copies of the document were made. One was to go to each of the states, and one was to be held by the national government. (When Vermont became the fourteenth state on March 4, 1791, another copy was made.)

Today, the federal government's copy is on display in the National Archives, a museum in Washington, D.C., not far from the Capitol. It is in an exhibit called the Charters of Freedom. Next to the Bill of Rights is an original copy of the Declaration of Independence and one of the U.S. Constitution.

Protecting the Bill of Rights

Even if you visit the National Archives, you won't be able to touch the actual Bill of Rights document. All the documents in the Charters of Freedom exhibit are protected in a special glass case. The glass is bulletproof to protect the document from would-be thieves. The case is also fireproof and has a

OTHER CONSTITUTIONAL AMMENDMENTS

Amendment XI

Passed by Congress March 4, 1794. Ratified February 7, 1795.

Note: Article III, section 2, of the Constitution was modified by Amendment 11.

The Judicial power of the United States shall not be construed to extend to any suit in law or equity, commenced or prosecuted against one of the United States by Citizens of another State, or by Citizens or Subjects of any Foreign State.

Amendment XII

Passed by Congress December 9, 1803. Ratified June 15, 1804.

Note: A portion of Article II, section 1 of the Constitution was superseded by the 12th amendment.

The Electors shall meet in their respective states and vote by ballot for President and Vice-President, one of whom, at least, shall not be an inhabitant of the same state with themselves; they shall name in their ballots the person voted for as President, and in distinct ballots the person voted for as Vice-President, and they shall make distinct lists of all persons voted for as President, and of all persons voted for as Vice-President, and of the number of votes for each, which lists they shall sign and certify, and transmit sealed to the seat of the government of the United States, directed to the President of the Senate; -- the President of the Senate shall, in the presence of the Senate and House of Representatives, open all the certificates and the votes shall then be counted; -- The person having the greatest number of votes for President, shall be the President, if such number be a majority of the whole number of Electors appointed; and if no person have such majority, then from the persons having the highest numbers not exceeding three on the list of those voted for as President, the House of Representatives shall choose immediately, by ballot, the President. But in choosing the President, the votes shall be taken by states, the representation from each state having one vote; a quorum for this purpose shall consist of a member or members from two-thirds of the states, and a majority of all the states shall be necessary to a choice. [And if the House of Representatives shall not choose a President whenever the right of choice shall devolve upon them, before the fourth day of March next following, then the Vice-President shall act as President, as in case of the death or other constitutional disability of the President. --]* The person having the greatest number of votes as Vice-President, shall be the Vice-President, if such number be a majority of the whole number of Electors appointed, and if no person have a majority, then from the two highest numbers on the list, the Senate shall choose the Vice-President; a quorum for the purpose shall consist of two-thirds of the whole number of Senators, and a majority of the whole number shall be necessary to a choice. But no person constitutionally ineligible to the office of President shall be eligible to that of Vice-President of the United States.

*Superseded by section 3 of the 20th Amendment.

Amendment XIII

Passed by Congress January 31, 1865. Ratified December 6, 1865.

Note: A portion of Article IV, section 2, of the Constitution was superseded by the 13th Amendment.

Section 1. Neither slavery nor involuntary servitude, except as a punishment for crime whereof the party shall have been duly convicted, shall exist within the United States, or any place subject to their jurisdiction.

Section 2. Congress shall have power to enforce this article by appropriate legislation.

Amendment XIV

Passed by Congress June 13, 1866. Ratified July 9, 1868.

Note: Article I, section 2, of the Constitution was modified by section 2 of the 14th Amendment.

Section 1. All persons born or naturalized in the United States, and subject to the jurisdiction thereof, are citizens of the United States and of the State wherein they reside. No State shall make or enforce any law which shall abridge the privileges or immunities of citizens of the United States; nor shall any State deprive any person of life, liberty, or property, without due process of law; nor deny to any person within its jurisdiction the equal protection of the laws.

Section 2. Representatives shall be apportioned among the several States according to their respective numbers, counting the whole number of persons in each State, excluding Indians not taxed. But when the right to vote at any election for the choice of electors for President and Vice-President of the United States, Representatives in Congress, the Executive and Judicial officers of a State, or the members of the Legislature thereof, is denied to any of the male inhabitants of such State, being twenty-one years of age,* and citizens of the United States, or in any way abridged, except for participation in rebellion, or other crime, the basis of representation therein shall be reduced in the proportion which the number of such male citizens shall bear to the whole number of male citizens twenty-one years of age in such State.

Section 3. No person shall be a Senator or Representative in Congress, or elector of President and Vice-President, or hold any office, civil or military, under the United States, or under any State, who, having previously taken an oath, as a member of Congress, or as an officer of the United States, or as a member of any State legislature, or as an executive or judicial officer of any State, to support the Constitution of the United States, shall have engaged in insurrection or rebellion against the same, or given aid or comfort to the enemies thereof. But Congress may by a vote of two-thirds of each House, remove such disability.

Section 4. The validity of the public debt of the United States, authorized by law, including debts incurred for payment of pensions and bounties for services in suppressing insurrection or rebellion, shall not be questioned. But neither the United States nor any State shall assume or pay any debt or obligation incurred in aid of insurrection or rebellion against the United States, or any claim for the loss or emancipation of any slave; but all such debts, obligations and claims shall be held illegal and void.

Section 5. The Congress shall have the power to enforce, by appropriate legislation, the provisions of this article.

*Changed by section 1 of the 26th Amendment.

Amendment XV

Passed by Congress February 26, 1869. Ratified February 3, 1870.

Section 1. The right of citizens of the United States to vote shall not be denied or abridged by the United States or by any State on account of race, color, or previous condition of servitude.

Section 2. The Congress shall have the power to enforce this article by appropriate legislation.

Amendment XVI

Passed by Congress July 2, 1909. Ratified February 3, 1913.

Note: Article I, section 9, of the Constitution was modified by Amendment 16.

The Congress shall have power to lay and collect taxes on incomes, from whatever source derived, without apportionment among the several States, and without regard to any census or enumeration.

Amendment XVII

Passed by Congress May 13, 1912. Ratified April 8, 1913.

Note: Article I, section 3, of the Constitution was modified by the 17th Amendment.

The Senate of the United States shall be composed of two Senators from each State, elected by the people thereof, for six years; and each Senator shall have one vote. The electors in each State shall have the qualifications requisite for electors of the most numerous branch of the State legislatures.

When vacancies happen in the representation of any State in the Senate, the executive authority of such State shall issue writs of election to fill such vacancies: Provided, That the legislature of any State may empower the executive thereof to make temporary appointments until the people fill the vacancies by election as the legislature may direct.

This amendment shall not be so construed as to affect the election or term of any Senator chosen before it becomes valid as part of the Constitution.

Amendment XVIII

Passed by Congress December 18, 1917. Ratified January 16, 1919. Repealed by Amendment 21.

Section 1. After one year from the ratification of this article the manufacture, sale, or transportation of intoxicating liquors within, the importation thereof into, or the exportation thereof from the United States and all territory subject to the jurisdiction thereof for beverage purposes is hereby prohibited.

Section 2. The Congress and the several States shall have concurrent power to enforce this article by appropriate legislation.

Section 3. This article shall be inoperative unless it shall have been ratified as an amendment to the Constitution by the legislatures of the several States, as provided in the Constitution, within seven years from the date of the submission hereof to the States by the Congress.

Amendment XIX

Passed by Congress June 4, 1919. Ratified August 18, 1920.

The right of citizens of the United States to vote shall not be denied or abridged by the United States or by any State on account of sex.

Congress shall have power to enforce this article by appropriate legislation.

Amendment XX

Passed by Congress March 2, 1932. Ratified January 23, 1933.

Note: Article I, section 4, of the Constitution was modified by section 2 of this amendment. In addition, a portion of the 12th Amendment was superseded by section 3.

Section 1. The terms of the President and the Vice President shall end at noon on the 20th day of January, and the terms of Senators and Representatives at noon on the 3d day of January, of the years in which such terms would have ended if this article had not been ratified; and the terms of their successors shall then begin.

Section 2. The Congress shall assemble at least once in every year, and such meeting shall begin at noon on the 3d day of January, unless they shall by law appoint a different day.

Section 3. If, at the time fixed for the beginning of the term of the President, the President elect shall have died, the Vice President elect shall become President. If a President shall not have been chosen before the time fixed for the beginning of his term, or if the President elect shall have failed to qualify, then the Vice President elect shall act as President until a President shall have qualified; and the Congress may by law provide for the case wherein neither a President elect nor a Vice President shall have qualified, declaring who shall then act as President, or the manner in which one who is to act shall be selected, and such person shall act accordingly until a President or Vice President shall have qualified.

Section 4. The Congress may by law provide for the case of the death of any of the persons from whom the House of Representatives may choose a President whenever the right of choice shall have devolved upon them, and for the case of the death of any of the persons from whom the Senate may choose a Vice President whenever the right of choice shall have devolved upon them.

Section 5. Sections 1 and 2 shall take effect on the 15th day of October following the ratification of this article.

Section 6. This article shall be inoperative unless it shall have been ratified as an amendment to the Constitution by the legislatures of three-fourths of the several States within seven years from the date of its submission.

Amendment XXI

Passed by Congress February 20, 1933. Ratified December 5, 1933.

Section 1. The eighteenth article of amendment to the Constitution of the United States is hereby repealed.

Section 2. The transportation or importation into any State, Territory, or Possession of the United States for delivery or use therein of intoxicating liquors, in violation of the laws thereof, is hereby prohibited.

Section 3. This article shall be inoperative unless it shall have been ratified as an amendment to the Constitution by conventions in the several States, as provided in the Constitution, within seven years from the date of the submission hereof to the States by the Congress.

Amendment XXII

Passed by Congress March 21, 1947. Ratified February 27, 1951.

Section 1. No person shall be elected to the office of the President more than twice, and no person who has held the office of President, or acted as President, for more than two years of a term to which some other person was elected President shall be elected to the office of President more than once. But this Article shall not apply to any person holding the office of President when this Article was proposed by Congress, and shall not prevent any person who may be holding the office of President, or acting as President, during the term within which this Article becomes operative from holding the office of President or acting as President during the remainder of such term.

Section 2. This article shall be inoperative unless it shall have been ratified as an amendment to the Constitution by the legislatures of three-fourths of the several States within seven years from the date of its submission to the States by the Congress.

Amendment XXIII

Passed by Congress June 16, 1960. Ratified March 29, 1961.

Section 1. The District constituting the seat of Government of the United States shall appoint in such manner as Congress may direct:

A number of electors of President and Vice President equal to the whole number of Senators and Representatives in Congress to which the District would be entitled if it were a State, but in no event more than the least populous State; they shall be in addition to those appointed by the States, but they shall be considered, for the purposes of the election of President and Vice President, to be electors appointed by a State; and they shall meet in the District and perform such duties as provided by the twelfth article of amendment.

Section 2. The Congress shall have power to enforce this article by appropriate legislation.

Amendment XXIV

Passed by Congress August 27, 1962. Ratified January 23, 1964.

Section 1. The right of citizens of the United States to vote in any primary or other election for President or Vice President, for electors for President or Vice President, or for Senator or

Representative in Congress, shall not be denied or abridged by the United States or any State by reason of failure to pay poll tax or other tax.

Section 2. The Congress shall have power to enforce this article by appropriate legislation.

Amendment XXV

Passed by Congress July 6, 1965. Ratified February 10, 1967.

Note: Article II, section 1, of the Constitution was affected by the 25th Amendment.

Section 1. In case of the removal of the President from office or of his death or resignation, the Vice President shall become President.

Section 2. Whenever there is a vacancy in the office of the Vice President, the President shall nominate a Vice President who shall take office upon confirmation by a majority vote of both Houses of Congress.

Section 3. Whenever the President transmits to the President pro tempore of the Senate and the Speaker of the House of Representatives his written declaration that he is unable to discharge the powers and duties of his office, and until he transmits to them a written declaration to the contrary, such powers and duties shall be discharged by the Vice President as Acting President.

Section 4. Whenever the Vice President and a majority of either the principal officers of the executive departments or of such other body as Congress may by law provide, transmit to the President pro tempore of the Senate and the Speaker of the House of Representatives their written declaration that the President is unable to discharge the powers and duties of his office, the Vice President shall immediately assume the powers and duties of the office as Acting President.

Thereafter, when the President transmits to the President pro tempore of the Senate and the Speaker of the House of Representatives his written declaration that no inability exists, he shall resume the powers and duties of his office unless the Vice President and a majority of either the principal officers of the executive department or of such other body as Congress may by law provide, transmit within four days to the President pro tempore of the Senate and the Speaker of the House of Representatives their written declaration that the President is unable to discharge the powers and duties of his office. Thereupon Congress shall decide the issue, assembling within forty-eight hours for that purpose if not in session. If the Congress, within twenty-one days after receipt of the latter written declaration, or, if Congress is not in session, within twenty-one days after Congress is required to assemble, determines by two-thirds vote of both Houses that the President is unable to discharge the powers and duties of his office, the Vice President shall continue to discharge the same as Acting President; otherwise, the President shall resume the powers and duties of his office.

Amendment XXVI

Passed by Congress March 23, 1971. Ratified July 1, 1971.

Note: Amendment 14, section 2, of the Constitution was modified by section 1 of the 26th Amendment.

Section 1. The right of citizens of the United States, who are eighteen years of age or older, to vote shall not be denied or abridged by the United States or by any State on account of age.

Section 2. The Congress shall have power to enforce this article by appropriate legislation.

Amendment XXVII

Originally proposed September 25, 1789. Ratified May 7, 1992.

No law, varying the compensation for the services of the Senators and Representatives, shall take effect, until an election of representatives shall have intervened.

BOOKS

Leavitt, Amie Jane. *The Bill of Rights in Translation: What It Really Means.* Mankato, MN: Capstone, 2008.

Sobel, Syl. *The Bill of Rights: Protecting Our Freedom Then and Now.* Hauppauge, New York: Barron's Educational Series, 2008.

Taylor-Butler, Christine. *The Bill of Rights.* New York: Scholastic, 2008.

Travis, Cathy. *Constitution Translated for Kids.* Austin, Texas: Ovation Books, 2008.

WORKS CONSULTED

ACLU of Texas: "Free Speech and the Right to Protest"
http://www.aclutx.org/2011/02/02/
free-speech-and-the-right-to-protest/

EyeWitness to History: "The Reichstag Fire. 1933,"
http://www.eyewitnesstohistory.com/reichstagfire.htm

First Amendment Center
http://www.firstamendmentcenter.org/

Freedom Forum
http://www.freedomforum.org/

Future of the First Amendment
http://firstamendmentfuture.org/

Grammaticas, Damian. "Chinese Woman Jailed Over Tweet." *BBC News,* November 18, 2010.
http://www.bbc.co.uk/news/world-asia-pacific-11784603

Library of Congress. *A Century of Lawmaking for a New Nation: U.S. Congressional Documents and Debates, 1774–1875.* Annals of Congress, House of Representatives, 1st Congress, 1st Session, pp. 441 and 442.
http://memory.loc.gov/cgi-bin/ampage?collId=llac&fileName=001/llac001.db&recNum=222

Library of Congress: Primary Documents in American History; The Bill of Rights
http://www.loc.gov/rr/program/bib/ourdocs/billofrights.html

National Archives. "National Archives Announces New Ban on
        Photography." January 26, 2010. http://www.archives.gov/press/
        press-releases/2010/nr10-53.html
National Archives: Preservation and Archives Professionals
        http://www.archives.gov/preservation/
Reporters Without Borders for Press Freedom
        http://en.rsf.org/
United Nations
        http://www.un.org/
United Nations: The Universal Declaration of Human Rights
        http://www.un.org/en/documents/udhr/
USA Today, "Freedom of Assembly," various dates and authors,
        http://www.usatoday.com/educate/college/casestudies/20061003-
        Assembly.pdf

ON THE INTERNET

Congress for Kids: The Bill of Rights
        http://www.congressforkids.net/games/billofrights/2_billofrights.htm
National Archives: Charters of Freedom
        http://www.archives.gov/exhibits/charters/
The White House: Our Government: The Constitution
        http://www.whitehouse.gov/our-government/the-constitution

amendment (uh-MEND-munt)—An official or formal change or addition to the Constitution.

Antifederalist (an-ty-FED-ruh-list)—A person who was against or had serious concerns about accepting the Constitution.

bail (BAYL)—Money that is left with a court to guarantee a person who is charged with a crime and set free will return for trial.

censor (SEN-sur)—To take out parts of a book, film, or other type of media to make it reflect political or religous beliefs.

communist (KAH-myoo-nist)—A person who believes in a form of government (communism) where all property is owned in common.

consensus (kun-SEN-sus)—An agreement.

constitution (kon-stih-TOO-shun)—A document that outlines the fundamental rules for a government.

delegate (DEH-lih-git)—A person chosen to act for or represent others.

double jeopardy (DUH-bul JEH-pur-dee)—The act of charging someone twice for the same crime.

Federalist (FEH-drul-ist)—A person who believed the Constitution should be accepted.

grand jury (GRAND JUR-ee)—A type of jury that determines whether there is enough evidence for a trial.

grievance (GREE-vunts)—A complaint.

jury (JUR-ee)—A group of people who listen to the facts of a court case and decide its outcome.

legislature (LEH-jis-lay-chur)—A group of elected people who make laws for the country.

libel (LY-bul)—Published words that are known to be untrue by the author and are meant to hurt another person.

Nazi (NAHT-zee)—A form of government in Germany that believed that one race of people was supreme to others and had the right to persecute those who were not part of that race.

peer (PEER)—A person of the same legal or social status as another.

petition (puh-TIH-shun)—To appeal something.

quarter (KWAR-tur)—To provide food and housing for another person.

ratification (rat-ih-fih-KAY-shun)—Official approval.

supersede (soo-per-SEED)—To take the place of something else.

tribunal (try-BYOO-nul)—A court.

verdict (VUR-dikt)—The outcome of a trial.

Antifederalists   6
Articles of Confederation   4
bail   30–31
Bill of Rights
     Amendment I   9, 10, 11, 12–13,
          16–17
     Amendment II   18, 20
     Amendment III   20–21
     Amendment IV   21–23
     Amendment V   24–25
     Amendment VI   26, 28
     Amendment VII   28–29
     Amendment VIII   30–31
     Amendment IX   31
     Amendment X   31
     ratification   9
     reasons for   7
     writing of   8
Borden, Lizzie   29
Charters of Freedom   32, 34
China   10–11, 16
Committee for the First Amendment,
     The   12
Congress   6, 8–9, 12–13, 17
Connecticut   9
Constitutional Convention   4
Constitution of the United States   4,
     6–9, 10, 12–15, 21, 23–24, 31–32, 37
cruel and unusual punishment   30
Declaration of Independence   32
Delaware   9
double jeopardy   25
English Bill of Rights   8
Federalists   6, 8
Franklin, Benjamin   4
French and Indian War   20
George III   6, 7, 17
Georgia   9
Germany   14–16, 23
grand jury   25
Hamilton, Alexander   4
Hitler, Adolf   14
Hollywood   12
Internet   13
Iran   16

Japan   10
jury   24–29
King, Rodney   24
King Kong   15
legislatures   8
libel   16, 17
Lord Baltimore   13
Madison, James   4, 8
Magna Carta   8
Maryland   9, 13
Mason, George   4, 8
Massachusetts   7, 9
National Archives   32, 33, 34
Nazis   14–16, 23
New Hampshire   9
New Jersey   9
New York   7, 9
North Carolina   7, 9
North Korea   16
Penn, William   13
Pennsylvania   9, 13
Pilgrims   13
public defender   28
public trial   28
Quakers   13
quartering   21
Reichstag   14
Reporters Without Borders   16
Revolutionary War   4, 5, 6, 17, 19
Rhode Island   7, 9
Roosevelt, Eleanor   36
search warrants   21–22
South Carolina   9
speedy trial   26, 28
United Nations   35–37
Universal Declaration of Human Rights
     35–37
verdict   29
Vermont   9, 32
Vietnam   16
Virginia   7, 8, 9
Virginia Declaration of Rights   8
Washington, D.C.   32–34
Washington, George   4
World War II   23, 35

ABOUT THE AUTHOR

Amie Jane Leavitt is an accomplished author and photographer. She graduated from Brigham Young University as an education major and has since taught all subjects and grade levels in both private and public schools. She is an adventurer who loves to travel the globe in search of interesting story ideas and beautiful places to capture on film. She has written dozens of books for kids, has contributed to online and print media, and has worked as a consultant, writer, and editor for numerous educational publishing and assessment companies. Amie has always had a great love for American law and history. One of her favorite memories is the first time she ever saw the original copy of the Bill of Rights in the National Archives when she was a senior in high school. To check out a listing of Amie's current projects and published works, visit her web site at http://www.amiejaneleavitt.com.